Grammaropolis PRESENTS

Wonderful Words
For Second Grade

VOCABULARY AND WRITING WORKBOOK

BY ORDER OF

The Mayor of Grammaropolis

Written by Christopher Knight
Interior Design by Christopher Knight
Cover Design by Mckee Frazior
Grammaropolis Character Design by Powerhouse Animation & Mckee Frazior

ISBN: 9781644420522
Copyright © 2021 by Grammaropolis LLC
All rights reserved.
Published by Six Foot Press
Printed in the U.S.A.

Grammaropolis.com
SixFootPress.com

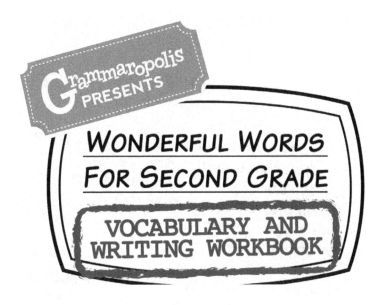

Grammaropolis PRESENTS

WONDERFUL WORDS
FOR SECOND GRADE

VOCABULARY AND
WRITING WORKBOOK

GRAMMAROPOLIS BOOKS

HOUSTON

FROM THE DESK OF THE MAYOR

Greetings, fellow wordsmith!

Thank you so much for using this workbook. I hope you have fun learning some new vocabulary words!

As you know, many words can act as multiple parts of speech; it all depends on how they're used in the sentence. For the sake of clarity and simplicity (and because we didn't have enough space on the page!), the definitions in this workbook include only one part of speech for each word.

It's great to know a lot of vocabulary words, but the real reason we expand our vocabulary is so that we can communicate more effectively. That's why I've added a writing exercise, with optional prompts, at the end of each section.

Thanks again for visiting Grammaropolis. I hope you enjoy your stay!

—The Mayor

TABLE OF CONTENTS

HOW TO USE THE VOCABULARY PAGES

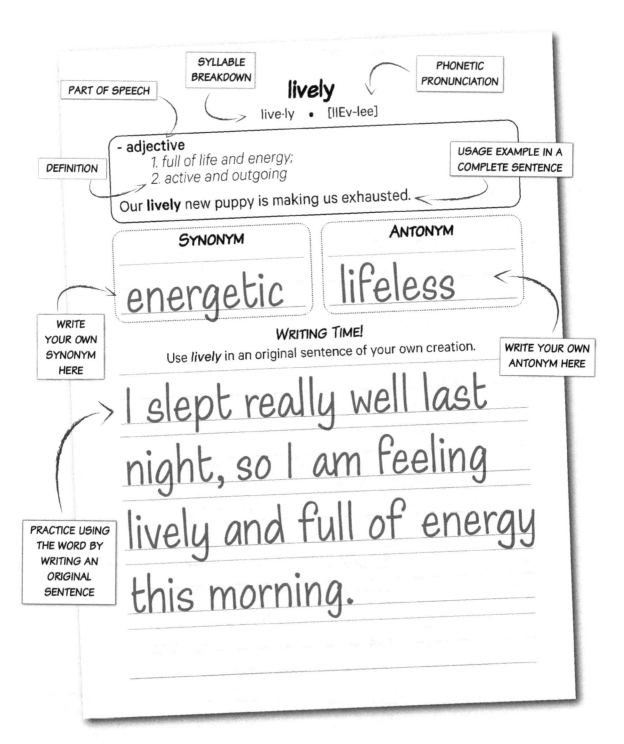

PART OF SPEECH

SYLLABLE BREAKDOWN

PHONETIC PRONUNCIATION

lively

live·ly • [llEv-lee]

DEFINITION

- adjective
1. full of life and energy;
2. active and outgoing

Our **lively** new puppy is making us exhausted.

USAGE EXAMPLE IN A COMPLETE SENTENCE

SYNONYM

energetic

ANTONYM

lifeless

WRITE YOUR OWN SYNONYM HERE

WRITE YOUR OWN ANTONYM HERE

WRITING TIME!
Use *lively* in an original sentence of your own creation.

PRACTICE USING THE WORD BY WRITING AN ORIGINAL SENTENCE

I slept really well last night, so I am feeling lively and full of energy this morning.

Important Note: Synonyms and antonyms for nouns might be harder to come up with than they are for verbs and adjectives, but do your best!

THE PARTS OF SPEECH REVIEW

Every word acts as at least one of the eight parts of speech. In this workbook, you'll find nouns, verbs, and adjectives. Here are some things you need to remember about them!

NOUNS

A noun can name a person, place, thing, or idea.

Naming a person:
Jason is my very best **friend**.

Naming a place:
Becks Prime is my favorite **restaurant**.

Naming a thing:
That **ball** is my favorite **toy**.

Naming an idea:
Honesty and **loyalty** are my best **qualities**.

VERBS

An action verb expresses mental or physical action, and a linking verb expresses a state of being.

Expressing physical action:
Richard **jumped** across the river.

Expressing mental action:
Richard **considered** jumping across the river.

Expressing a state of being:
Richard **feels** bad. He **is** sorry for jumping across the river.

ADJECTIVES

*An adjective modifies a noun or a pronoun and tells **what kind, which one, how much,** or **how many**.*

Modifying a noun:
The **quick brown** fox jumped over the **enormous red** fence at the **first** sign of trouble.

Modifying a pronoun:
They are **satisfied** with the answer, but I am still **curious**.

There are five other parts of speech you won't find in this workbook, but that doesn't mean they're not important!

ADVERBS

*An adverb modifies a verb, an adjective, or another adverb and tells **how, where, when,** or **to what extent**.*

PRONOUNS

A pronoun takes the place of one or more nouns or pronouns.

CONJUNCTIONS

A conjunction joins words or word groups.

PREPOSITIONS

A preposition shows a logical relationship or locates an object in time or space.

INTERJECTIONS

An interjection expresses strong or mild emotion.

SECTION ONE: WORD PREVIEW
Welcome to your eight new favorite words!

When you encounter a new word, take a moment to consider what it might mean.

1. Think about the word and circle what part of speech you think it is. (*Many words can act as more than one part of speech, depending on how they're used in the sentence, **so only choose one part of speech below.***)

2. Come up with a brief definition of the word in the part of speech you've chosen. It doesn't have to be the *correct* definition—just do your best.

classify
Part of Speech: noun   verb   adjective

Definition:_____

_____

similar
Part of Speech: noun   verb   adjective

Definition:_____

_____

sum
Part of Speech: noun   verb   adjective

Definition:_____

_____

helpful
Part of Speech: noun   verb   adjective

Definition:_____

_____

greedy
Part of Speech: noun   verb   adjective

Definition:_____

_____

insist
Part of Speech: noun   verb   adjective

Definition:_____

_____

process
Part of Speech: noun   verb   adjective

Definition:_____

_____

agree
Part of Speech: noun   verb   adjective

Definition:_____

_____

classify

clas·si·fy • [klAs-uh-fie]

- verb

    1. to group into a class, classification, or category

At lunch I always **classify** my food according to color.

Synonym	Antonym

Writing Time!

Use *classify* in an original sentence of your own creation.

_____

_____

_____

_____

_____

_____

_____

similar

sim·i·lar • [slm-uh-luhr]

- adjective

1. having characteristics in common : very much alike

Jake doesn't have that exact jacket, but he has a **similar** one.

SYNONYM	ANTONYM

WRITING TIME!

Use *similar* in an original sentence of your own creation.

sum

sum • [sUHm]

- noun
1. *an indefinite or specified amount of money;*
2. *the whole amount : an existent total*

The **sum** of all our spare change is enough to buy one cookie.

SYNONYM	ANTONYM

WRITING TIME!
Use *sum* in an original sentence of your own creation.

_____

_____

_____

_____

_____

_____

helpful

help·ful • [hElp-fuhl]

- adjective

   1. of service or assistance: useful

It's always **helpful** when you hold the door open for someone.

SYNONYM	ANTONYM

WRITING TIME!

Use *helpful* in an original sentence of your own creation.

greedy

greed·y • [grEE-dee]

- adjective

1. having or showing an intense and selfish desire for something, especially wealth or power

Please stop being so **greedy** and share your candy.

SYNONYM	ANTONYM

WRITING TIME!

Use *greedy* in an original sentence of your own creation.

insist

in·sist • [in-sIst]

- verb

1. to take a stand and refuse to give way : hold firmly to something

Jacqueline didn't want to walk the dog, but her mom **insisted**.

SYNONYM	ANTONYM

WRITING TIME!

Use *insist* in an original sentence of your own creation.

_____

_____

_____

_____

_____

_____

_____

_____

process

pro·cess • [prAH-ses]

- **noun**

   1. a series of actions or steps taken in order to achieve a particular end

Do you know the **process** for building a robot?

SYNONYM	ANTONYM

WRITING TIME!

Use *process* in an original sentence of your own creation.

_____

_____

_____

_____

_____

_____

_____

_____

agree

a·gree • [uh-grEE]

- verb

   1. to concur in (as an opinion)

Jenny and Val always **agree** on what to eat because they have the same taste in food.

SYNONYM

_____

_____

_____

ANTONYM

_____

_____

_____

WRITING TIME!

Use *agree* in an original sentence of your own creation.

_____

_____

_____

_____

_____

_____

_____

_____

SECTION ONE: WORD REVIEW

Congratulations on learning eight amazing new words! Remember that the whole point of learning new vocabulary is actually to use it, so let's put your new vocabulary to use.

1. Review the words you've learned. Consider what ideas come to mind when you say the words. How about when you read the definitions?

2. Circle at least **two** of your favorites. You'll get to use these when you write your very own story!

classify —————— verb
1. *to group into a class, classification, or category*

similar —————— adjective
1. *having characteristics in common : very much alike*

sum —————— noun
1. *an indefinite or specified amount of money;*
2. *the whole amount : an existent total*

helpful —————— adjective
1. *of service or assistance: useful*

greedy —————— adjective
1. *having or showing an intense and selfish desire for something, especially wealth or power*

insist —————— verb
1. *to take a stand and refuse to give way : hold firmly to something*

process —————— noun
1. *a series of actions or steps taken in order to achieve a particular end.*

agree —————— verb
1. *to concur in (as an opinion)*

STORY ONE

1. List the words you've chosen:

_____

2. Write a story that incorporates all of your chosen words. If you can't think of anything to write about, consider these suggestions:
   - Write a story that takes place inside a restaurant.
   - Write a story that begins, "I knew this was a bad idea."

_____

_____
_____

_____
_____

_____
_____

_____
_____

_____

Wonderful Words for Second Grade Vocabulary & Writing Workbook ©2021 Grammaropolis LLC

Wonderful Words for Second Grade Vocabulary & Writing Workbook ©2021 Grammaropolis LLC

Section Two: Word Preview
Welcome to your eight new favorite words!

When you encounter a new word, take a moment to consider what it might mean.

1. Think about the word and circle what part of speech you think it is. *(Many words can act as more than one part of speech, depending on how they're used in the sentence, **so only choose one part of speech below.**)*

2. Come up with a brief definition of the word in the part of speech you've chosen. It doesn't have to be the *correct* definition—just do your best.

drowsy
Part of Speech: noun verb adjective

Definition:_____

_____

parade
Part of Speech: noun verb adjective

Definition:_____

_____

dangerous
Part of Speech: noun verb adjective

Definition:_____

_____

diagram
Part of Speech: noun verb adjective

Definition:_____

_____

pale
Part of Speech: noun verb adjective

Definition:_____

_____

annoy
Part of Speech: noun verb adjective

Definition:_____

_____

moist
Part of Speech: noun verb adjective

Definition:_____

_____

nervous
Part of Speech: noun verb adjective

Definition:_____

_____

drowsy

drows·y • [drOU-zee]

- adjective

    1. sleepy and lethargic

I'm so **drowsy** that I can hardly keep my eyes open.

SYNONYM

ANTONYM

WRITING TIME!

Use *drowsy* in an original sentence of your own creation.

parade

pa·rade • [puhr-rAYd]

> **- noun**
>   *1. a march or procession;*
>   *2. a pompous show : formal display*
>
> The city threw a big **parade** to celebrate the team's victory.

SYNONYM	ANTONYM

WRITING TIME!

Use *parade* in an original sentence of your own creation.

_____

_____

_____

_____

_____

_____

_____

_____

dangerous

dan·ger·ous • [dAYn-juhr-ruhs]

- **adjective**
  1. *exposing to danger;*
  2. *involving risk*

Playing with matches is really **dangerous**.

SYNONYM	ANTONYM

WRITING TIME!
Use *dangerous* in an original sentence of your own creation.

diagram

di·a·gram • [dIE-uh-gram]

- noun

1. a simplified drawing showing the appearance, structure, or workings of something

Can you draw Kyla a **diagram** of an English catapult?

SYNONYM	ANTONYM

WRITING TIME!
Use *diagram* in an original sentence of your own creation.

pale

pale • [pAYl]

- adjective
    1. deficient in color or in intensity or depth of color;
    2. dusky white

That **pale** curtain isn't nearly bright or colorful enough for me.

SYNONYM	ANTONYM

WRITING TIME!
Use *pale* in an original sentence of your own creation.

annoy

an·noy • [uh-nOY]

- verb
    1. *to irritate*

It **annoys** me when you poke me in the nose repeatedly.

SYNONYM

ANTONYM

WRITING TIME!
Use *annoy* in an original sentence of your own creation.

moist

moist • [mOIst]

- **adjective**
    1. *slightly wet;*
    2. *damp or humid*

My t-shirt was supposed to dry overnight, but it's still **moist**.

SYNONYM	ANTONYM

WRITING TIME!

Use *moist* in an original sentence of your own creation.

nervous

ner·vous • [nUHR-vuhs]

- adjective
    1. *easily agitated or alarmed;*
    2. *tending to be anxious*

Calm down and don't be **nervous**! That snake isn't venomous.

SYNONYM	ANTONYM

WRITING TIME!

Use *nervous* in an original sentence of your own creation.

_____

_____

_____

_____

_____

_____

_____

_____

_____

_____

SECTION TWO: WORD REVIEW

Congratulations on learning eight amazing new words! Remember that the whole point of learning new vocabulary is actually to use it, so let's put your new vocabulary to use.

1. Review the words you've learned. Consider what ideas come to mind when you say the words. How about when you read the definitions?

2. Circle at least **two** of your favorites. You'll get to use these when you write your very own story!

drowsy —————— adjective
1. sleepy and lethargic

parade —————— noun
1. a march or procession;
2. a pompous show : formal display

dangerous ——— adjective
1. exposing to danger;
2. involving risk

diagram —————— noun
1. a simplified drawing showing the appearance, structure, or workings of something

pale —————— adjective
1. deficient in color or in intensity or depth of color;
2. dusky white

annoy —————— verb
1. to irritate

moist —————— adjective
1. slightly wet;
2. damp or humid

nervous —————— adjective
1. easily agitated or alarmed
2. tending to be anxious

STORY TWO

1. List the words you've chosen:

_____

2. Write a story that incorporates all of your chosen words. If you can't think of anything to write about, consider these suggestions:
   - Write a story that takes place in the year 2400.
   - Write a story in which the only type of food available is anchovy ice cream.

_____

_____
_____

_____
_____

_____
_____

_____
_____

_____
_____

Wonderful Words for Second Grade Vocabulary & Writing Workbook ©2021 Grammaropolis LLC

SECTION THREE: WORD PREVIEW
Welcome to your eight new favorite words!

When you encounter a new word, take a moment to consider what it might mean.

1. Think about the word and circle what part of speech you think it is.
   (*Many words can act as more than one part of speech, depending on how they're used in the sentence, **so only choose one part of speech below.***)

2. Come up with a brief definition of the word in the part of speech you've chosen. It doesn't have to be the *correct* definition—just do your best.

gather
Part of Speech: noun verb adjective

Definition:_____

_____

core
Part of Speech: noun verb adjective

Definition:_____

_____

famous
Part of Speech: noun verb adjective

Definition:_____

_____

skill
Part of Speech: noun verb adjective

Definition:_____

_____

shelter
Part of Speech: noun verb adjective

Definition:_____

_____

cycle
Part of Speech: noun verb adjective

Definition:_____

_____

team
Part of Speech: noun verb adjective

Definition:_____

_____

gaze
Part of Speech: noun verb adjective

Definition:_____

_____

gather

gath·er • [gA-THuhr]

- verb
    1. to bring together into a crowd, group, body, or mass;
    2. to summon up : muster together

Please **gather** some wildflowers so we can make a bouquet.

SYNONYM	ANTONYM

WRITING TIME!
Use *gather* in an original sentence of your own creation.

core

core • [kOR]

- noun
> *1. the central or most important part of something*

The **core** of a baseball is actually made out of cork.

SYNONYM	ANTONYM

WRITING TIME!
Use *core* in an original sentence of your own creation.

famous

fa·mous • [fAY-muhs]

- adjective

1. much talked about : well- known

That donut shop is **famous**! The whole school knows about it.

SYNONYM	ANTONYM

WRITING TIME!

Use *famous* in an original sentence of your own creation.

skill

skill • [skɪl]

- noun

1. a developed or acquired aptitude or ability

Archery requires **skill** that you have to practice all the time.

SYNONYM	ANTONYM

WRITING TIME!

Use *skill* in an original sentence of your own creation.

shelter

shel·ter • [shEl-tuhr]

- **noun**
    1. something that provides refuge from danger;
    2. a means or place of protection

I found **shelter** from the rain underneath an old bridge.

SYNONYM	ANTONYM

WRITING TIME!
Use *shelter* in an original sentence of your own creation.

_____

_____

_____

_____

_____

_____

_____

_____

cycle

cy·cle • [sIE-kuhl]

- noun

1. the period of time taken to complete a single sequence of events

The life **cycle** of a fruit fly is only 24 hours!

SYNONYM	ANTONYM

WRITING TIME!

Use *cycle* in an original sentence of your own creation.

team

team • [tEEm]

- noun

1. two or more people associated together in work or activity

You can't do that by yourself! You need to join a **team** instead.

SYNONYM	ANTONYM
_____	_____
_____	_____

WRITING TIME!

Use *team* in an original sentence of your own creation.

_____

_____

_____

_____

_____

_____

_____

_____

gaze

gaze • [gAYz]

- **verb**

   1. to look with eagerness (as in admiration or wonder) or with studious attention

   Howie **gazed** at the gorgeous stars for hours last night.

Synonym	Antonym

Writing Time!

Use *gaze* in an original sentence of your own creation.

SECTION THREE: WORD REVIEW

Congratulations on learning eight amazing new words! Remember that the whole point of learning new vocabulary is actually to use it, so let's put your new vocabulary to use.

1. Review the words you've learned. Consider what ideas come to mind when you say the words. How about when you read the definitions?

2. Circle at least **two** of your favorites. You'll get to use these when you write your very own story!

gather ——— verb
1. to bring together into a crowd, group, body, or mass;
2. to summon up : muster together

core ——— noun
1. the central or most important part of something

famous ——— adjective
1. much talked about : well-known

skill ——— noun
1. a developed or acquired aptitude or ability

shelter ——— noun
1. something that provides refuge from danger;
2. a means or place of protection

cycle ——— noun
1. the period of time taken to complete a single sequence of events

team ——— noun
1. two or more people associated together in work or activity

gaze ——— verb
1. to look with eagerness (as in admiration or wonder) or with studious attention

STORY THREE

1. List the words you've chosen:

_____

2. Write a story that incorporates all of your chosen words. If you can't think of anything to write about, consider these suggestions:
   - **Write a story that takes place during a rainstorm.**
   - **Write a story in which your main character has super speed.**

_____

_____
_____

_____
_____

_____
_____

_____
_____

Wonderful Words for Second Grade Vocabulary & Writing Workbook ©2021 Grammaropolis LLC

SECTION FOUR: WORD PREVIEW
Welcome to your eight new favorite words!

When you encounter a new word, take a moment to consider what it might mean.

1. Think about the word and circle what part of speech you think it is.
   *(Many words can act as more than one part of speech, depending on how they're used in the sentence, **so only choose one part of speech below.**)*

2. Come up with a brief definition of the word in the part of speech you've chosen. It doesn't have to be the *correct* definition—just do your best.

— safe —
Part of Speech: noun   verb   adjective

*Definition:*_____

_____

— warn —
Part of Speech: noun   verb   adjective

*Definition:*_____

_____

— reflect —
Part of Speech: noun   verb   adjective

*Definition:*_____

_____

— friendly —
Part of Speech: noun   verb   adjective

*Definition:*_____

_____

— design —
Part of Speech: noun   verb   adjective

*Definition:*_____

_____

— whisper —
Part of Speech: noun   verb   adjective

*Definition:*_____

_____

— atlas —
Part of Speech: noun   verb   adjective

*Definition:*_____

_____

— curious —
Part of Speech: noun   verb   adjective

*Definition:*_____

_____

safe

safe • [sAYf]

- **adjective**

1. secure from threat of danger, harm, or loss

Sarah's money isn't **safe** in the shoe box beneath her bed.

SYNONYM	ANTONYM

WRITING TIME!

Use *safe* in an original sentence of your own creation.

warn

warn • [wORn]

- verb

  1. to inform in advance of an impending or possible danger, problem, or other unpleasant situation

Jamie **warned** me that it would be sunny, so I packed a hat!

SYNONYM

_____

_____

ANTONYM

_____

_____

WRITING TIME!

Use *warn* in an original sentence of your own creation.

_____

_____

_____

_____

_____

_____

_____

_____

_____

reflect

re·flect • [ri-flEkt]

> **- verb**
> 1. (of a mirror or shiny surface) to show an image of;
> 2. to think deeply or carefully about
>
> The shiny glass **reflected** my smile right back to me.

SYNONYM	ANTONYM

WRITING TIME!
Use *reflect* in an original sentence of your own creation.

_____

_____

_____

_____

_____

_____

_____

_____

friendly

friend·ly • [frEHnd-lee]

- **adjective**
  1. kind and pleasant

Bobby Jo is a **friendly** person who is fun to play with.

SYNONYM	ANTONYM

WRITING TIME!

Use *friendly* in an original sentence of your own creation.

_____

_____

_____

_____

_____

_____

_____

_____

_____

_____

design

de·sign • [di-zIEn]

- verb

1. to conceive and plan out something

Let's **design** a machine that serves us cake every hour.

SYNONYM

ANTONYM

WRITING TIME!

Use *design* in an original sentence of your own creation.

whisper

whis·per • [wIs-puhr]

- verb
>   1. *to speak softly with little or no vibration of the vocal cords*

When you **whisper** like that, I can't hear a word you're saying.

SYNONYM	ANTONYM

WRITING TIME!
Use *whisper* in an original sentence of your own creation.

atlas

at·las • [At-luhs]

- noun

1. a book of maps or charts

Sergei bought a new **atlas** because he loves looking at maps.

SYNONYM	ANTONYM
_____	_____
_____	_____

WRITING TIME!

Use *atlas* in an original sentence of your own creation.

_____

_____

_____

_____

_____

_____

_____

_____

_____

curious

cu·ri·ous • [kyUR-ee-uhs]

- adjective

1. marked by desire to investigate and learn : showing interest in finding or searching out information

The **curious** little boy wouldn't stop asking questions.

SYNONYM	ANTONYM

WRITING TIME!

Use *curious* in an original sentence of your own creation.

SECTION FOUR: WORD REVIEW

Congratulations on learning eight amazing new words! Remember that the whole point of learning new vocabulary is actually to use it, so let's put your new vocabulary to use.

1. Review the words you've learned. Consider what ideas come to mind when you say the words. How about when you read the definitions?
2. Circle at least **two** of your favorites. You'll get to use these when you write your very own story!

safe ———— adjective
1. secure from threat of danger, harm, or loss

warn ———— verb
1. to inform in advance of an impending or possible danger, problem, or other unpleasant situation

reflect ———— verb
1. (of a shiny surface) to show an image of;
2. to think deeply or carefully about

friendly ———— adjective
1. kind and pleasant

design ———— verb
1. to conceive and plan out something

whisper ———— verb
1. to speak softly with little or no vibration of the vocal cords

atlas ———— noun
1. a book of maps or charts

curious ———— adjective
1. marked by desire to investigate and learn : showing interest in finding or searching out information

STORY FOUR

1. List the words you've chosen:

_____

2. Write a story that incorporates all of your chosen words. If you can't think of anything to write about, consider these suggestions:
   - **Write a story about a bright orange puppy.**
   - **Write a story that takes place in an enormous city park.**

_____

_____
_____

_____
_____

_____
_____

_____
_____

_____

Wonderful Words for Second Grade Vocabulary & Writing Workbook ©2021 Grammaropolis LLC

Wonderful Words for Second Grade Vocabulary & Writing Workbook ©2021 Grammaropolis LLC

SECTION FIVE: WORD PREVIEW
Welcome to your eight new favorite words!

When you encounter a new word, take a moment to consider what it might mean.

1. Think about the word and circle what part of speech you think it is.
   *(Many words can act as more than one part of speech, depending on how they're used in the sentence, **so only choose one part of speech below**.)*

2. Come up with a brief definition of the word in the part of speech you've chosen. It doesn't have to be the *correct* definition—just do your best.

doubt
Part of Speech: noun   verb   adjective

*Definition:*_____

_____

alive
Part of Speech: noun   verb   adjective

*Definition:*_____

_____

connect
Part of Speech: noun   verb   adjective

*Definition:*_____

_____

support
Part of Speech: noun   verb   adjective

*Definition:*_____

_____

worry
Part of Speech: noun   verb   adjective

*Definition:*_____

_____

deep
Part of Speech: noun   verb   adjective

*Definition:*_____

_____

settle
Part of Speech: noun   verb   adjective

*Definition:*_____

_____

bare
Part of Speech: noun   verb   adjective

*Definition:*_____

_____

doubt

doubt • [dOUt]

- verb

    1. to lack confidence in : distrust, suspect

I **doubt** that you can jump directly onto the roof.

SYNONYM	ANTONYM

WRITING TIME!

Use *doubt* in an original sentence of your own creation.

alive

a·live • [uh-LIEv]

- **adjective**
    1. having life : not dead

    My sister thought butterfly was dead, but it was still **alive**!

SYNONYM	ANTONYM

WRITING TIME!
Use *alive* in an original sentence of your own creation.

_____

_____

_____

_____

_____

_____

_____

connect

con·nect • [kuh-nEkt]

- **verb**
  1. to join, fasten, or link together

  If you **connect** these two ropes, you will have one long rope.

SYNONYM	ANTONYM

WRITING TIME!

Use *connect* in an original sentence of your own creation.

_____

_____

_____

_____

_____

_____

_____

_____

_____

_____

_____

support

sup·port • [suh-pORt]

- verb
> *1. to bear all or part of the weight of : hold up;*
> *2. to give assistance to*

The main wall **supports** the whole ceiling, so don't remove it.

SYNONYM	ANTONYM

WRITING TIME!
Use *support* in an original sentence of your own creation.

worry

wor·ry • [wUHR-ree]

- verb

  1. to afflict with mental distress or agitation : make anxious

Don't **worry** about missing class; I will take notes for you.

SYNONYM	ANTONYM
_____	_____
_____	_____

WRITING TIME!

Use *worry* in an original sentence of your own creation.

_____

_____

_____

_____

_____

_____

_____

_____

_____

deep

deep • [dEEp]

- adjective
    1. *extending far down from the top or surface;*
    2. *very intense or extreme*

Be very careful when wading through **deep** water.

SYNONYM	ANTONYM

WRITING TIME!
Use *deep* in an original sentence of your own creation.

settle

set·tle • [sEt-l]

- **verb**
    1. *to establish in residence;*
    2. *to change from disturbance to tranquility*

My grandparents **settled** in a nice spot at a bend in the river.

SYNONYM	ANTONYM

WRITING TIME!
Use *settle* in an original sentence of your own creation.

bare

bare • [bAIR]

- **adjective**
    1. *lacking a covering;*
    2. *exposed or open to view*

Miguel's **bare** arms were cold when the winter wind gusted.

SYNONYM	ANTONYM

WRITING TIME!

Use *bare* in an original sentence of your own creation.

_____

_____

_____

_____

_____

_____

_____

_____

SECTION FIVE: WORD REVIEW

Congratulations on learning eight amazing new words! Remember that the whole point of learning new vocabulary is actually to use it, so let's put your new vocabulary to use.

1. Review the words you've learned. Consider what ideas come to mind when you say the words. How about when you read the definitions?
2. Circle at least **two** of your favorites. You'll get to use these when you write your very own story!

doubt ——— verb
1. to lack confidence in : distrust, suspect

alive ——— adjective
1. having life : not dead

connect ——— verb
1. to join, fasten, or link together

support ——— verb
1. to bear all or part of the weight of : hold up;
2. to give assistance to

worry ——— verb
1. to afflict with mental distress or agitation : make anxious

deep ——— adjective
1. extending far down from the top or surface;
2. very intense or extreme

settle ——— verb
1. to establish in residence;
2. to change from disturbance to tranquility

bare ——— adjective
1. lacking a covering;
2. exposed or open to view

STORY FIVE

1. List the words you've chosen:

_____

2. Write a story that incorporates all of your chosen words. If you can't think of anything to write about, consider these suggestions:

   - **Write a story in which your main character is you ten years from now.**
   - **Write a story that takes place in an amusement park.**

_____

_____
_____

_____
_____

_____
_____

_____
_____

_____

Wonderful Words for Second Grade Vocabulary & Writing Workbook ©2021 Grammaropolis LLC

Wonderful Words for Second Grade Vocabulary & Writing Workbook ©2021 Grammaropolis LLC

SECTION SIX: WORD PREVIEW
Welcome to your eight new favorite words!

When you encounter a new word, take a moment to consider what it might mean.

1. Think about the word and circle what part of speech you think it is. *(Many words can act as more than one part of speech, depending on how they're used in the sentence, **so only choose one part of speech below.**)*

2. Come up with a brief definition of the word in the part of speech you've chosen. It doesn't have to be the *correct* definition—just do your best.

tremble
Part of Speech: noun   verb   adjective

*Definition:*_____

_____

frighten
Part of Speech: noun   verb   adjective

*Definition:*_____

_____

planet
Part of Speech: noun   verb   adjective

*Definition:*_____

_____

lonely
Part of Speech: noun   verb   adjective

*Definition:*_____

_____

escape
Part of Speech: noun   verb   adjective

*Definition:*_____

_____

expect
Part of Speech: noun   verb   adjective

*Definition:*_____

_____

steady
Part of Speech: noun   verb   adjective

*Definition:*_____

_____

treasure
Part of Speech: noun   verb   adjective

*Definition:*_____

_____

tremble

trem·ble • [trEm-buhl]

- **verb**

    1. to shake involuntarily (as with fear, cold, excitement, or fatigue)

Our little puppy's legs **trembled** when the big dog walked by.

SYNONYM	ANTONYM

WRITING TIME!

Use *tremble* in an original sentence of your own creation.

_____

_____

_____

_____

_____

_____

_____

_____

_____

frighten

fright·en • [frIEt-n]

- **verb**
  1. to markedly disturb with fear : make afraid

  Enormous snakes **frighten** me more than just about anything.

SYNONYM

ANTONYM

WRITING TIME!
Use *frighten* in an original sentence of your own creation.

planet

plan·et • [plAn-uht]

- **noun**

1. *a celestial body moving in an elliptical orbit around a star*

My favorite **planet** is Mercury because it's closest to the sun.

SYNONYM	ANTONYM

WRITING TIME!

Use *planet* in an original sentence of your own creation.

lonely

lone·ly • [lOHn-lee]

- **adjective**
  1. dejected and unhappy as a result of being alone

  Natasha felt **lonely** when nobody was around to play with her.

SYNONYM	ANTONYM

WRITING TIME!
Use *lonely* in an original sentence of your own creation.

_____

_____

_____

_____

_____

_____

_____

_____

_____

escape

es·cape • [i-skAYp]

- verb

1. to break free from confinement or control

Benny's dog somehow **escaped** from the back yard.

SYNONYM	ANTONYM

WRITING TIME!

Use *escape* in an original sentence of your own creation.

expect

ex·pect • [ik-spEkt]

- verb

  1. to look forward to : look ahead with anticipation

I **expect** that my teacher will give us more time for recess.

SYNONYM	ANTONYM

WRITING TIME!

Use *expect* in an original sentence of your own creation.

_____

_____

_____

_____

_____

_____

_____

_____

_____

steady

stead·y • [stEd-ee]

- adjective

1. firm in standing or position : not tottering or shaking

Be sure your hand is **steady** or you'll spill the water all over.

SYNONYM	ANTONYM

WRITING TIME!

Use *steady* in an original sentence of your own creation.

_____

_____

_____

_____

_____

_____

_____

_____

treasure

trea·sure • [trEzh-uhr]

- **noun**

  1. *a quantity of precious metals, gems, or other items of great value*

  The **treasure** of my dreams is basically a box of gold bricks.

SYNONYM	ANTONYM

WRITING TIME!

Use *treasure* in an original sentence of your own creation.

SECTION SIX: WORD REVIEW

Congratulations on learning eight amazing new words! Remember that the whole point of learning new vocabulary is actually to use it, so let's put your new vocabulary to use.

1. Review the words you've learned. Consider what ideas come to mind when you say the words. How about when you read the definitions?

2. Circle at least **two** of your favorites. You'll get to use these when you write your very own story!

tremble ———— verb
1. to shake involuntarily (as with fear, cold, excitement, or fatigue)

frighten ———— verb
1. to markedly disturb with fear : make afraid

planet ———— noun
1. a celestial body moving in an elliptical orbit around a star

lonely ———— adjective
1. dejected and unhappy as a result of being alone

escape ———— verb
1. to break free from confinement or control

expect ———— verb
1. to look forward to : look ahead with anticipation

steady ———— adjective
1. firm in standing or position : not tottering or shaking

treasure ———— noun
1. a quantity of precious metals, gems, or other items of great value

STORY SIX

1. List the words you've chosen:

_____

2. Write a story that incorporates all of your chosen words. If you can't think of anything to write about, consider these suggestions:
   - **Write a story starring your teacher as a pirate captain.**
   - **Write a story that takes place in a world where cars fly and horses talk.**

_____

_____
_____

_____
_____

_____
_____

_____
_____

_____

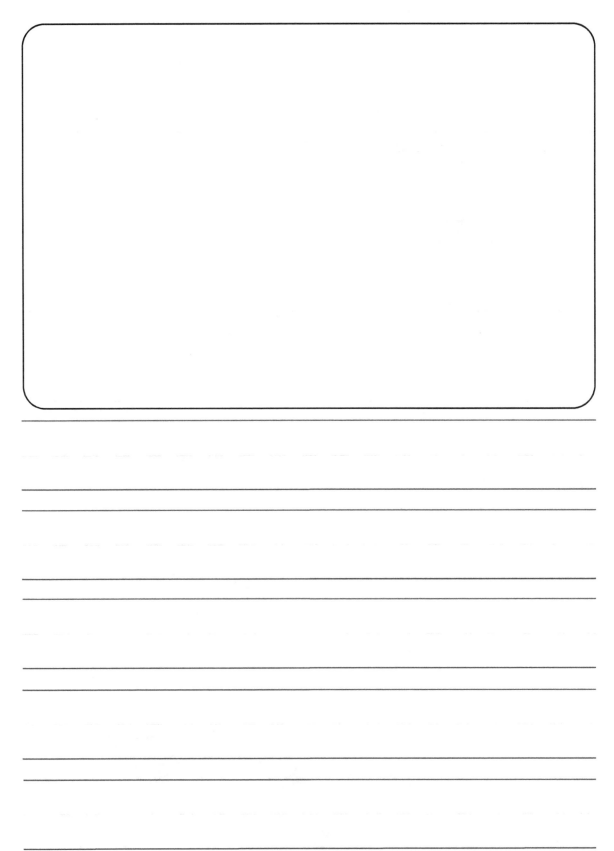

Wonderful Words for Second Grade Vocabulary & Writing Workbook ©2021 Grammaropolis LLC

INDEX OF WORDS USED